Crystal Cathedral Golden Collection

Edited by Mark Thallander

FOREWORD

The singing of hymns is as old as Christendom. Hymns are the music of the congregation, and can always be a part of worship when no other music is available.

While they can be effectively sung *a cappella*, a fine organ to accompany them and encourage congregational singing has been a priority of my husband's and mine throughout our ministry, and especially during these fifty years in Garden Grove.

When I became the first organist of this church, now known as the Crystal Cathedral, we had only a small electronic organ. Over the years, larger and finer organs were acquired. The world-famous Hazel Wright Organ was dedicated in the Crystal Cathedral in 1982. The outstanding organists who have led us in worship over these years have been a blessing not only to our congregation, but also to untold numbers of others through the *Hour of Power* televised service each week. We have frequently been asked for the arrangements our organists have used, as they are specifically for congregational accompaniment rather than solo organ pieces.

This collection contains previously published *and* new accompaniments. They are presented in this 50th Anniversary collection with the hope that they will continue to lead and inspire congregations as they lift their voices in praise of our Lord and Savior, Jesus Christ.

Arvella Schuller

Table of Contents

1963-1984

Richard Unfried is a native of Inglewood, California, and holds the title *Professor of Music Emeritus* at Biola University where he retired from the faculty in 1998, having taught pipe organ performance and music theory there for 41 years. He is a graduate of the University of Southern California, and has studied organ with Robert Prichard, Irene Robertson, and Clarence Mader. He was a finalist in the 1969 National Organ Playing Competition at Fort Wayne, Indiana.

Mr. Unfried has enjoyed fifty-three years of uninterrupted service as organist for Southern California churches including twenty-one years at the Crystal Cathedral. As organist for the Robert Schuller Ministries and the Crystal Cathedral, he performed in over 500 internationally televised *Hour of Power* broadcasts from 1970 through 1982.

Richard has enjoyed a long association with the American Guild of Organists, having served the Orange County Chapter as Dean. He has been a featured recitalist at several AGO Conventions. Additionally, he serves on the Board of the *Ruth and Clarence Mader Memorial Scholarship Fund*, and is a member of the American Society of Composers, Authors, and Publishers (ASCAP). His books, *Organ Hymns of Praise from the Crystal Cathedral* (Fred Bock Music Co.) and *Hymn Exultations for Organ* (Hinshaw Music, Inc.), are used by organists in more than 10,000 American churches.

Richard and Yvonne Unfried have two sons and two grandchildren.

1976-1993

Mark Thallander joined The Crystal Cathedral Music Ministry staff in 1976. He served as an associate to Don G. Fontana and assisted Arvella Schuller with Hour of Power television scripting, service programming and musical guests. During his 18 year tenure at the church, Mark assisted both Richard Unfried and Fred Swann with the playing responsibilities for the many services, seasonal concerts and the Glory of Christmas and Glory of Easter pageants, as well as recording projects. As Assistant Director of Music and Organist, Mark conducted both The Cathedral Choir and The Summer Choir on many occasions when Mr. Swann was away on concert tours. Mark coordinated the choir of 1,000 voices for the gala dedication of the Hazel Wright Organ and participated in the 10th anniversary celebration.

Mark accepted an invitation to serve as Associate Minister of Worship at Menlo Park Presbyterian Church, Menlo Park, California, in the Fall of 1993. He was able to take the many ideas he had learned from worship experiences at The Crystal Cathedral and share them with other congregations. For three years he was Director of Music and Organist at Lake Avenue Congregational Church, Pasadena. Most recently while Mark was Assistant Professor of Music at Vanguard University of Southern California, Costa Mesa, he was Organist at Glendale Presbyterian Church for three years, as well as assisting with the Cathedral's Christmas and Easter pageants.

His organ arrangements are published by Fred Bock Music Companies, where he is an organ editor, and he also reviews organ music for Creator Magazine. Mark has served as clinician and organist for national music conferences and church conventions, and has held offices in the American Guild of Organists, including Dean of the Orange County Chapter.

1982-1998

Frederick Swann, Organist Emeritus of the Crystal Cathedral and the First Congregational Church of Los Angeles, is Organ Artist-in-Residence at St. Margaret's Episcopal Church in Palm Desert, California. Since 2002, he has been President of the American Guild of Organists. During his long and illustrious career Mr. Swann has played recitals in many of the major churches, cathedrals and concert halls throughout North America and Europe, as well as in Asia and South America. He has also appeared frequently as soloist with leading orchestral and choral organizations. For 25 years Mr. Swann was Director of Music and Organist of the famed Riverside Church in New York City, and held the same title at the Crystal Cathedral for 16 years, where he was chief musician for the Hour of Power telecast viewed by millions throughout the world each week. Also known as a teacher, workshop leader, competition adjudicator, composer and recording artist, Mr. Swann still performs a limited number of recitals each season.

1998-2004

Hailed as one of today's leading young organists by critics on both sides of the Atlantic, **J. Christopher Pardini** maintains an active concert schedule as a concert organist both in the United States and abroad. Serving as Organist and Director of Music at Shadyside Presbyterian Church in Pittsburgh, Pennsylvania, Mr. Pardini heads one of the nation's leading church music programs. In this capacity he also serves as Artistic Director of *Music in a Great Space*, the church's concert series.

Mr. Pardini earned the Bachelor of Music degree in Sacred Music from Westminster Choir College in Princeton, NJ where he was an organ student of Donald McDonald and Eugene Roan. He also earned the Master of Music degree in Organ Performance and Literature from the Eastman School of Music in Rochester, NY where he was a student of David Higgs. The first-place winner in the 1998 San Marino Organ Competition, in San Marino, CA, Mr. Pardini has also studied organ with Kenrick Mervine and Gavin Black, and organ improvisation with Gerre Hancock. In addition, Mr. Pardini has also studied voice with Paulo Faustini and Tracy Chebra, and choral conducting with James Jordan and Andrew Magill.

Before coming to Pittsburgh, Mr. Pardini served as Senior Organist at the Crystal Cathedral in Garden Grove, California where he presided over the 17,000 pipe Hazel Wright Organ for the *Hour of Power* telecast. While at the Crystal Cathedral, he performed weekly to an estimated twenty million television viewers around the world. While in California, Mr. Pardini also served on the Board of Directors of the Clarence Mader Scholarship Fund. Mr. Pardini is also active as a composer of works for choir, organ, and orchestra. His music is published by G.I.A. in Chicago, Illinois.

2003-Present

Sean Groombridge, Minister of Worship and Senior Organist, joined the Cathedral staff in 2003 after serving in several churches in Canada; most recently at Benton Street Baptist Church, Kitchener, Ontario from 1998 to 2003. Sean received his Master of Music degree in Conducting/Church music from Northwestern University, Evanston, Il., where he also studied organ with Margaret Kemper and Wolfgang Rübsam. His undergraduate degree in Sacred Music/Organ and Composition was earned at the Moody Bible Institute of Chicago, under Dr. Elizabeth Naegele. While in Chicago, Sean and his wife, Beth, interned and served in the music ministries at the historic Moody Memorial Church and toured with the Moody Chorale. In recent years Sean has led various international music ministry tours and hosted Sacred Music workshops in Canada and the United States. Serving as Minister of Worship at Crystal Cathedral, Sean gives oversight to and directs Praise Teams, choral and instrumental ensembles, and assists in programming and co-ordination of Sunday services and special events.

The Hazel Wright Organ was built by Fratelli Ruffatti in Padua, Italy. The Ruffatti organ that was installed in the former sanctuary of the church in 1977 was combined with the Aeolian-Skinner organ formerly in the Avery Fisher Hall at The Lincoln Center for the Performing Arts in New York City. Several new divisions were provided by Ruffatti.

The concept and original design of the Hazel Wright Organ was by the legendary organist Virgil Fox. His untimely death before the installation resulted in changes and additions supervised by Frederick Swann over a ten year period. This work was effected by the Curators of the Organ who have cared for it beginning with the installation: Guy Henderson, John Wilson, and Brian Sawyers. The Organ, one of the ten largest in the world, is the third largest church organ in America.

Complete details and specifications on the Hazel Wright Organ, and other organs at the Cathedral, may be found in The Organs and the Carillon of the Crystal Cathedral, available from the Crystal Cathedral bookstore.

A Mighty Fortress Is Our God

(EIN' FESTE BURG)

Martin Luther

Arranged by Frederick Swann

To Final Stanza
fff
Solo
Interlude
ff
L.H.
R.H.
L.H.
rit.
Final Stanza
Ped.
rit.

All Creatures of Our God and King

(LASST UNS ERFREUEN)

Geistliche Kirchengesäng
Arranged by Richard Unfr

Interlude
Stanza 2
(Amen)
Solo Reed
Gt:

All Hail the Power of Jesus' Name

(CORONATION)

Oliver Holden
Arranged by Frederick Swann

Interlude
molto rit.
a tempo
Gt.
ff
Final Stanza
Trumpet
Trumpet
Trumpet

All People Who On Earth Do Dwell

(OLD HUNDREDTH)

I. = 16′ through Mix.
II. = Solo Trumpet 8′, 4′

Attributed to Louis Bourgeois
Arranged by Frederick Swann

*Note: If an interlude is desired use the introduction, beginning with the 3rd beat of the introduction as the <u>downbeat</u> of the final measure of the verse.

**Note: Depending upon the text sung, you may use A or B in either order, whichever seems appropriate.

Amazing Grace! How Sweet the Sound

(AMAZING GRACE)

"Virginia Harmony," 183

Arranged by Mark Thallander

Stanzas
Interlude
Final Stanza

Angels, from the Realms of Glory

(REGENT SQUARE)

Henry T. Smart
Arranged by Mark Thallander

Joyfully ♩= 100

Introduction

Interlude

Broadly
Final stanza

Come, Christians, Join to Sing

(MADRID)

Traditional Spanish Melody
Arranged by Mark Thallander

Interlude

Final Stanza

Come, O Long-Expected Jesus

(HYFRYDOL)

Rowland H. Prichard
Arranged by Frederick Swann

Interlude
Solo Trumpet
Pedal tacet
no rit.
add Pedal
Gt.
ff
Final Stanza
+16′
+32′

Come, O Almighty King

(ITALIAN HYMN)

Felice de Giardini

Arranged by Richard Unfried

Rev. and Mrs. Robert H. Schuller are seen here on Sunday, March 27, 1955 as they prepare to leave their small home to conduct their first worship service at the Orange Drive-in Theater. The church's electronic organ - played by Mrs. Schuller - is on the trailer.

Crown Him with Many Crowns

(DIADEMATA)

I. = Principal Chorus
II. = Reeds 16′, 8′, 4′

George J. Elvey
Arranged by Frederick Swann

To Final Stanza
Very marcato
Interlude
Final Stanza
Marcato
I.
II.
non legato
I.
rit.
cresc.
+32′

Fairest Lord Jesus

(CRUSADER'S HYMN)

Silesian Folk Melody
Arranged by Mark Thallander

To Next Stanza
Interlude
Stanzas
1.
To Final Stanza
Interlude

Final Stanza

Richard Unfried, who served as organist for twenty years, is pictured in the congregation's former sanctuary, now known as The Arboretum.

For the Beauty of the Earth

(DIX)

Conrad Kocher
Arranged by Mark Thallander

Interlude

Final Stanza

Hazel Wright with Dr. and Mrs. Schuller
at the Gala premiere Concert, May 7, 1982.

God of Grace and God of Glory

(CWM RHONDDA)

John Hughes

Arranged by Richard Unfried

Hark! The Herald Angels Sing

(MENDELSSOHN)

Felix Mendelssohn
Arranged by Mark Thallander

Interlude to Final Stanza
Tpts.
Gt.
Final Stanza
Tpts.
Tpts.
+32'

Holy, Holy, Holy! Lord God Almighty

(NICAEA)

John B. Dykes

Arranged by Mark Thallander

2 Interlude
Final Stanza

I Love Your Kingdom, Lord

(ST. THOMAS)

Aaron Williams
Arranged by Sean Groombridge

Stanza 3
mf
Manuals only
Interlude to Final Stanza
Trumpets
Ped.
Broadening to a stately tempo
Final Stanza
Trumpets

I Sing the Mighty Power of God

(ELLACOMBE)

"Gesangbuch der Herzogl," 1784

Arranged by Mark Thallander

Interlude
Final Stanza

In the Cross of Christ I Glory

(RATHBUN)

Ithamar Conkey
Arranged by Frederick Swann

1.
2. To Final Stanza
Interlude
rit.
Final Stanza
ff
poco rit.

In Christ There Is No East or West

(ST. PETER)

Alexander R. Reinagle
Arranged by Richard Unfrie

Frederick Swann is pictured with Alicia,
one of the stars of the world famous Glory of Easter Pageant.

Jesus Is All the World to Me

(ELIZABETH)

Will L. Thompson
Arranged by Mark Thallander

Interlude

Final Stanza

Jesus Shall Reign

(DUKE STREET)

John Hatton
Arranged by Frederick Swann

To Final Stanza
Interlude
rit.
a tempo
Final Stanza
rit.
Big Reed

Joyful, Joyful, We Adore You

(HYMN TO JOY)

I. = 16′ through Mix.
II.= Solo Trumpet 8′, 4′

Ludwig van Beethoven
Arranged by Frederick Swann

1.
To Final Stanza
+Reeds
Interlude
marcato
rit.
Final Stanza
sim.
Ped.
rit.

Lead On, O King Eternal

(LANCASHIRE)

Henry T. Smart
Arranged by Mark Thallander

Introduction

1.
To Final Stanza
Trumpets
Interlude
Final Stanza

Love Divine, All Loves Excelling

(BEECHER)

John Zundel
Arranged by Richard Unfrie

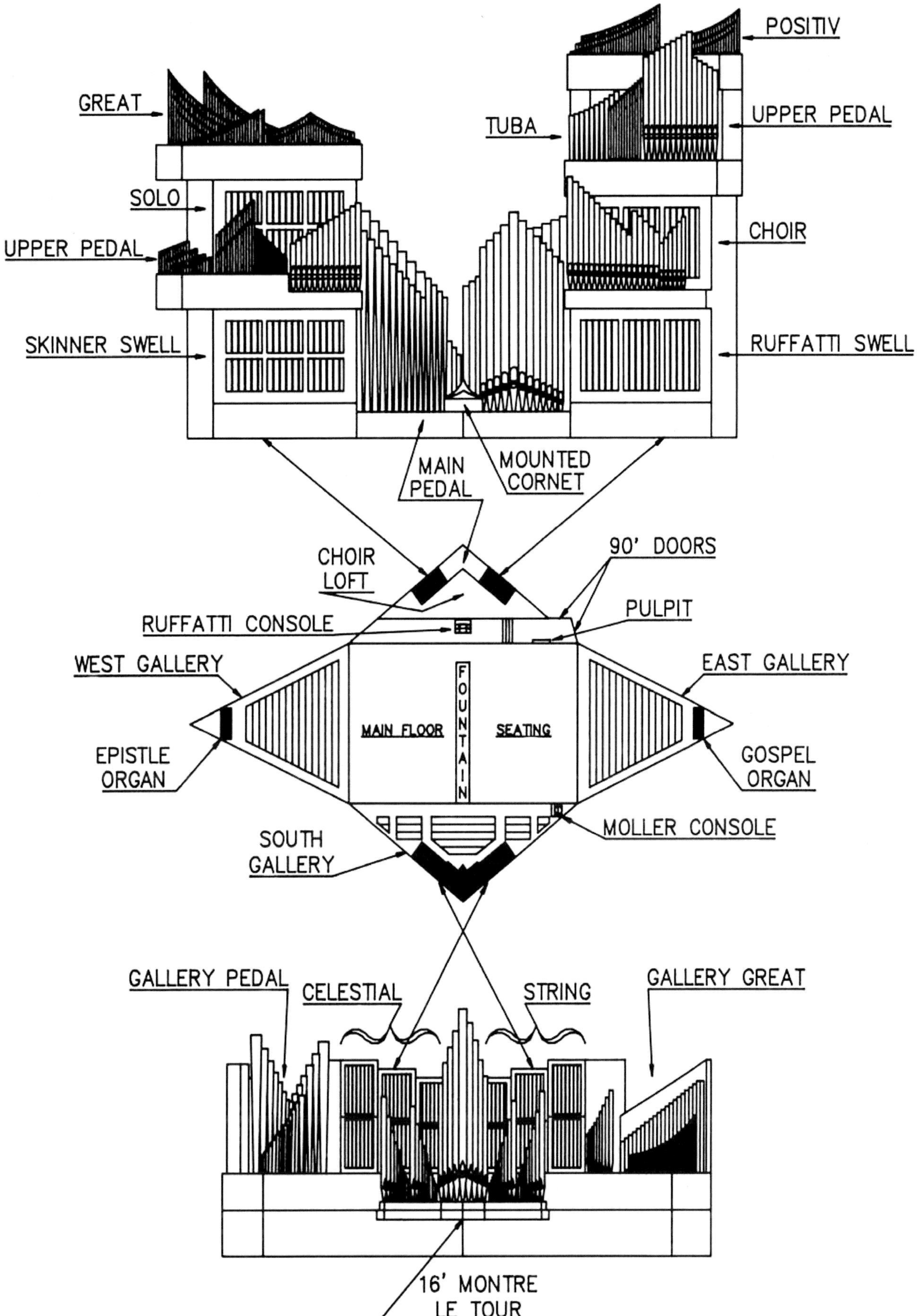

THE DISPERSED LOCATIONS OF THE ORGAN'S 12 DIVISIONS

My Country, 'Tis of Thee

(AMERICA)

Thesaurus Musicus, 1744
Arranged by J. Christopher Pardini

26
1.
2.
Interlude to Final Stanza
Trumpets
Gt.
31
35
Final Stanza
39
Tpts.
44
Gt.
+32'
rit.

No, Not One!

(NO, NOT ONE)

George C. Hugg
Arranged by Mark Thallander

Interlude

Final Stanza

Now Thank We All Our God

(NUN DANKET)

Johann Cruger
Arranged by Frederick Swann

1.
To Final Stanza
Solo Trumpet
Interlude
rit.
Final
Stanza
a tempo
Ped.

O Come, All Ye Faithful

(ADESTE FIDELES)

John F. Wade's *Cantus Divers*
Arranged by Richard Unfried

Interlude
simile
Stanza 2
Man.
Ped.

O For a Thousand Tongues to Sing

(AZMON)

I. = Principal Chorus
II. = Large Reeds 8′, 4′

Carl G. Glaser
Arranged by Frederick Swann

Interlude
II. Marcato
Stanza 3
I.
Ped.
Interlude
II. Marcato
I.
Full Organ
Stanza 4
+32′

O God, Our Help in Ages Past

(ST. ANNE)

William Croft
Arranged by Frederick Swann

To Final Stanza
Interlude
Large Reed
rit.
Final Stanza
+32′ Reed
-32′Reed
Ped.
Large Reed
rit.

O Master, Let Me Walk with You

(MARYTON)

H. Percy Smith
Arranged by Mark Thallander

Stanza
Interlude
Final Stanza

O Worship the King

(LYONS)

Johann Michael Haydn
Arranged by Mark Thallander

Majestically ♩ = 112

*If used, omit the last measure and molto ritard in the system above.

O Little Town of Bethlehem

(ST. LOUIS)

Lewis H. Redner

Arranged by Richard Unfrie

Gala Premiere Concert, May 7, 1982.
Pierre Cochereau, organist, Jean-Marc Cochereau, conductor,
with symphony orchestra and a choir of 1,000 voices.

Praise to the Lord, the Almighty

(LOBE DEN HERREN)

"Stralsund Gesangbuch"
Arranged by Frederick Swann

To Final Stanza
Interlude
Solo Trumpet
Final Stanza
Gt.
Solo Trumpet
Full Organ
add 32′
Gt.
Ped.

Praise the Lord! O Heavens, Adore Him

(AUSTRIAN HYMN)

Franz Joseph Haydn
Arranged by Mark Thallander

Victoriously ♩ = 100

Introduction

Interlude
trumpets
Broadly
Final stanza

poco a poco cresc.
ff
molto rit.

Mark Challander at the South Balcony console.
Tenth anniverssary of the Hazel Wright Organ.

Rejoice, the Lord Is King

(DARWALL'S 148th)

John Darwall
Arranged by Frederick Swann

Interlude
Freely
+16′
rit.
a tempo
Final Stanza
rit.

Rise Up, O Church of God!

(FESTAL SONG)

William H. Walter
Arranged by Mark Thallander

1
2
Interlude
Final Stanza

Sing Praise to God Who Reigns Above

(MIT FREUDEN ZART)

Bohemian Brethren's *Kirchengesänge*, 1566
Arranged by Mark Thallander

Interlude
Final stanza
ff
molto rit.

Stand Up, Stand Up for Jesus

(WEBB)

George J. Webb

Arranged by Frederick Swann

Principals 16′
rit.
Final Stanza
Solo Trumpet
+32′
-32′
Marcato
Ped.
rit.

The Solid Rock

(SOLID ROCK)

William B. Bradbury
Arranged by Mark Thallander

Introduction

Stanzas

To Final Stanza
Interlude
Final Stanza
Ped.

The Lord's My Shepherd

(CRIMOND)

Jessie S. Irvine
Arranged by Richard Unfried

There's a Wideness In God's Mercy

(WELLESLEY)

Lizzie S. Tourjee
Arranged by Frederick Swann

This Is My Father's World

(TERRA BEATA)

English Melody

Arranged by Mark Thallander

Final Stanza

To God Be the Glory

(TO GOD BE THE GLORY)

William H. Doane
Arranged by J. Christopher Pardini

28
34
40
46
52
1.
2.
To Final Stanza
Interlude
Trumpets
56
Gt.

61
Final Stanza
67
73
79
Trumpets
Gt.
84
Trumpets
Gt.
90

J. Christopher Pardini served as Organist of the Crystal Cathedral from 1996 though 2004.

We Praise You, O God, Our Redeemer, Creator

(KREMSER)

Netherlands Folk Song
Arranged by Mark Thallander

Interlude
trumpets
Final stanza
ff

We've a Story to Tell to the Nations

(MESSAGE)

H. Ernest Nichol
Arranged by Mark Thallander

Sean Groombridge, seen here at the Hazel Wright Organ after his first Sunday morning service in 2004, is the current Organist at the Crystal Cathedral.

What a Friend We Have In Jesus

(CONVERSE)

Charles C. Converse

Arranged by Mark Thallander

Interlude
Final Stanza

The five rank Mounted Cornet is situated like a jewel amid 32' and 16' Pedal pipes. This French-Classic inspired compound stop is a solo voice of uncommon power and beauty, composed of flue pipes of the following pitches: 8', 4', 2-2/3', 2', and 1-3/5'.

What Child Is This?

(GREENSLEEVES)

English Melody
Arranged by Richard Unfried

When Morning Gilds the Skies

(LAUDES DOMINI)

Joseph Barnby
Arranged by Frederick Swann

1.
To Final Stanza
Interlude
Add Organ
Full Pedal
Final Stanza
Solo Trumpet
rit.

While Shepherds Watched Their Flocks

(CHRISTMAS)

George Friedrich Handel

Arranged by Richard Unfried